FOREX TRADING

**Basics Guide
Geo Report
2023**

Chapter 1: Introduction to Forex Trading

1. What is Forex Trading?

Forex Trading: Exploring the World of Forex

In the vast financial universe, a frequently mentioned term is "Forex Trading". Its importance transcends borders and nations, directly influencing global markets. The origin of the term is the very essence of this market: "Forex" derives from the combination of the words "Foreign Exchange", which in Portuguese means "Foreign Exchange". It represents the market where currencies from different countries are exchanged at constantly fluctuating exchange rates.

What is Forex Trading?

At its core, Forex Trading involves buying and selling currencies. The main objective is to profit from fluctuations in exchange rates between different currencies. Imagine that you are planning a trip abroad and need to exchange your local currency for the currency of the country you are going to visit. In this exchange process, you are participating in a transaction on the Forex market on a smaller scale.

However, Forex Trading goes far beyond travel transactions. It has become one of the largest and most liquid financial markets in the world. Trillions of dollars are traded daily on this market, surpassing the combined volume of all other financial markets. This is due to the global nature of currencies and the interconnectedness of economies.

Fluctuations in Exchange Rates and Profit

The core idea behind Forex Trading is to take advantage of fluctuations in exchange rates. Exchange rates are influenced by a number of factors, including economic indicators, geopolitical events and changes in countries' monetary policies. When you anticipate an appreciation of one currency against another, you can buy that currency at a lower price and sell it when its value increases, profiting from the difference.

Liquidity and Accessibility

Liquidity is one of the main reasons why Forex Trading is so attractive to traders all over the world. Due to its massive size, it is possible to execute high volume trades without significantly compromising exchange rates. Furthermore, Forex is accessible 24 hours a day, five days a week due to the global nature of the market and different time zones.

Forex Trading is the art of trading currencies in search of profit through fluctuations in exchange rates. The term "Forex" encapsulates the essential nature of this market, which is the exchange of foreign currencies. With its exceptional liquidity and global influence, Forex Trading offers exciting opportunities for traders of all experience levels.

2. Why is Forex Trading popular?

The Reasons Behind the Popularity of Forex Trading

Forex Trading has gained significant popularity on the global financial scene, attracting traders from all corners of the world. This popularity is no accident; it is based on several distinct characteristics that make the Forex market so attractive and accessible. Let's explore the main reasons behind this phenomenon.

1. High Liquidity: The Heart of the Market

High liquidity is one of the most outstanding features of Forex Trading. The Forex market is colossal, with a daily trading volume that exceeds trillions of dollars. This means that there are always plenty of buyers and sellers ready to transact. This liquidity reduces the risk of large price movements due to a single trade and allows traders to execute their orders with ease.

2. Schedule Flexibility: 24 Hours of Opportunities

Forex Trading takes place 24 hours a day, Monday through Friday. This is due to the global nature of the market, which spans time zones from different parts of the world. This flexibility allows traders from different locations and time zones to find trading opportunities at any time, making Forex a truly continuous market.

3. Accessibility for All

The Forex market is known to be accessible to individuals with different levels of capital. Thanks to the evolution of technology, online trading platforms have allowed even traders with small investments to participate. Many brokerages offer trading accounts with minimal lot sizes, making it possible for virtually anyone to enter the market.

4. Possibility of Leverage

Leverage is a feature that allows traders to control positions larger than their available capital. While it is a powerful tool for amplifying gains, it also carries a higher level of risk. The possibility of leverage attracts traders looking for opportunities for higher profits, even with relatively modest initial investments.

5. Global Nature and Diversity

The global nature of the Forex market is one of the main factors behind its popularity. Currency is an integral part of international transactions and trade relations between countries. This means that a wide range of participants, including individuals, multinational companies and financial institutions, are involved in the Forex market, creating an environment rich in diversity and opportunities.

The popularity of Forex Trading is rooted in its high liquidity, flexible hours, accessibility, leverage potential and global nature. These features combined have created a dynamic and accessible environment for traders of all experience levels, making Forex Trading a popular choice in the investment world.

3. Differences between Forex and other financial markets

Differences between the Forex Market and Other Financial Markets

The Forex market stands out as one of the most unique and distinctive financial markets as compared to other markets such as stocks and commodities. These differences are rooted in the characteristics of each market and the asset classes that are traded.

1. Focus on Currency Trading

The main difference lies in the focus of traded assets. While Forex Trading is centered around buying and selling currency pairs such as EUR/USD (Euro/US Dollar) or USD/JPY (US Dollar/Japanese Yen), other markets involve diverse assets such as stocks of companies, physical commodities (gold, oil) and even financial derivatives.

2. Global Nature and Diversification

The Forex market is truly global due to the nature of currencies and international trade. It transcends borders and is influenced by economic and political events in different countries. On the other hand, equity and commodity markets have their own regional and sectoral characteristics, which create opportunities for diversification.

3. Abundant Liquidity

One of the main advantages of the Forex market is its high liquidity. With daily trading volumes exceeding trillions of dollars, Forex is known for its ability to execute high volume transactions without significantly affecting exchange rates. By comparison, equity and commodity markets can have varying levels of liquidity, depending on the asset and the timing.

4. Powerful Leverage

Forex also stands out for the possibility of significant leverage. Traders can control positions larger than their starting capital, amplifying both potential gains and losses. In equity and commodity markets, leverage is generally lower and can vary depending on the asset and market regulations.

5. Schedule Flexibility

Another notable difference is the flexibility of Forex market hours. Operating 24 hours a day, five days a week, Forex allows traders to access the market across different time zones. In contrast, stock and commodity markets have tighter trading hours and are often closed during weekends.

The Forex market stands out for currency trading as its main focus, its global nature, high liquidity, affordable leverage and flexible hours. These characteristics distinguish it from equity and commodity markets, which involve a diverse range of assets and have different levels of liquidity, leverage and trading hours. Each market has its own advantages and challenges, serving different profiles of traders and investors.

4. Major Forex Market Players

Forex Market Participants: A Complex Dance of Influences

The Forex market is a complex ecosystem, where diverse participants interact to shape fluctuations in exchange rates and the ongoing functioning of the market. Each group plays a crucial role, reflecting the specific interests and objectives of your financial operations.

Let's explore the key players and how their interactions impact this dynamic market.

1. Central Banks

Central banks play a central role in the Forex market. They are responsible for formulating and implementing a country's monetary policy. By adjusting interest rates and taking steps to control the money supply, central banks can directly influence the value of the national currency. Their actions are often visible in monetary policy announcements and currency interventions.

2. Financial Institutions

Commercial banks, investment funds and other financial institutions are also active participants in the Forex market. They trade currencies on behalf of clients, pursue arbitrage opportunities and manage the risks associated with currency fluctuations. These institutions can influence exchange rates through their large transactions, especially when operating in significant volumes.

3. Multinational Companies

Multinational companies are directly involved in international trade and therefore in the Forex market. They use Forex to convert foreign currencies into their local currency, managing currency risks associated with international operations. Their activities impact the demand for different currencies and can influence exchange rates.

4. Individual Traders

Individual traders, often referred to as retail traders, are an increasingly important player in the Forex market. With the availability of online trading platforms, anyone with internet access can get in on the game. While individual volumes may be smaller, taken together, individual traders can affect short-term fluctuations and contribute to market liquidity.

5. Institutional Investors

Institutional investors such as pension funds and hedge funds also operate in the Forex market. They often seek global diversification and hedging against currency risks. Your investments in foreign currencies can be significant, especially when looking for long-term opportunities in specific markets.

The Dance of Influence on Exchange Rates

The interaction between these participants creates a dynamic ecosystem where exchange rates are determined by a number of factors, including supply and demand, economic indicators, geopolitical events and changes in monetary policies. Actions by central banks, for example, can have immediate impacts on exchange rates, while the commercial activities of multinational companies have more gradual effects.

The complex dance of influences between these players shapes the Forex market, making it an arena where diverse strategies and different objectives meet. Understanding these interactions is critical for any trader or investor wishing to successfully navigate this ever-moving market.

5. Advantages and Disadvantages of Forex Trading

Balanced Analysis of the Advantages and Disadvantages of Forex Trading

Forex Trading offers exciting opportunities, but it also brings with it significant challenges. A balanced analysis of the advantages and disadvantages helps to understand the pros and cons of this dynamic market.

Benefits:

1. High Liquidity: The high liquidity of the Forex market allows traders to easily execute buy and sell orders, preventing slippage and improving transaction efficiency.

2. Currency Pair Diversification: With a vast array of currency pairs to choose from, traders have the ability to diversify their strategies and exposure to different economies.

3. Accessibility: Forex is accessible to a wide range of traders, regardless of available capital. This allows traders with different investment levels to enter the market.

4. Leverage: Leverage allows traders to control positions larger than their equity, potentially amplifying profits. This can be advantageous if used with caution.

Disadvantages:

1. Volatility Risk: Exchange rate volatility can be intense and unpredictable. While volatility can lead to profitable opportunities, it also increases the risk of substantial losses.

2. Excessive Leverage: While leverage is a powerful tool, overuse can amplify losses and lead to margin calls, where traders can lose more than they initially invested.

3. Sensitivity to Global Events: The Forex market is sensitive to geopolitical, economic and social events around the world. Unexpected changes can result in sudden movements in exchange rates.

4. Decentralized Market: Unlike centralized markets like the stock market, the Forex market is decentralized, which can result in a lack of regulation and transparency in some areas.

Forex Trading is a journey that offers notable advantages such as high liquidity, pair diversification, accessibility and leverage. However, these advantages come with inherent disadvantages, including volatility risks, excessive leverage and sensitivity to global events. To successfully navigate the Forex market, traders must have a solid understanding of the unique characteristics of this market and a disciplined approach to risk management.

Chapter 2: Forex Market Basics

1. Major, minor and exotic currency pairs

Currency Pairs in the Forex Market: Major, Minor and Exotic

In the Forex market, currency pairs are the essence of transactions, representing exchange rates between different currencies. There are three main categories of currency pairs: majors, minors and exotics. Each of these categories reflects different levels of liquidity, volatility and popularity.

1. Major Currency Pairs:

Major currency pairs are the most traded and widely recognized in the Forex market. They represent major global economies and involve the strongest and most traded currencies. The US dollar (USD) is often present in major pairs, due to its role as the world's reserve currency. Examples of major currency pairs include:

- EUR/USD: Euro (EUR) against US dollar (USD)
- USD/JPY: US Dollar (USD) against Japanese Yen (JPY)
- GBP/USD: Pound Sterling (GBP) against the US Dollar (USD)
- USD/CHF: US Dollar (USD) against Swiss Franc (CHF)

2. Secondary Currency Pairs:

Minor currency pairs, also known as "minor pairs", do not include the US dollar. They are made up of currencies from developed economies, but which are not as influential as major currencies. Some examples of secondary currency pairs are:

- EUR/GBP: Euro (EUR) against British Pound (GBP)
- AUD/JPY: Australian Dollar (AUD) against Japanese Yen (JPY)
- NZD/CAD: New Zealand Dollar (NZD) against Canadian Dollar (CAD)

3. Exotic Currency Pairs:

Exotic currency pairs involve a major currency and a currency from an emerging or lesser known economy. They often have lower liquidity and trading volume compared to major and minor pairs, which can result in higher volatility. Examples of exotic currency pairs include:

- USD/SGD: US Dollar (USD) against Singapore Dollar (SGD)
- EUR/TRY: Euro (EUR) against Turkish Lira (TRY)
- USD/THB: US Dollar (USD) versus Thai Baht (THB)

Currency pairs in the Forex market are grouped into three main categories: majors, minors and exotics. Each category reflects different currency combinations and liquidity levels. Major currency pairs represent the most influential economies, minor pairs include currencies from smaller economies, and exotic pairs involve currencies from emerging or lesser known economies. The choice of currency pairs depends on each trader's trading goals and risk tolerance.

2. Currency quotes and pips

Currency Quotes and Forex Pips: Crucial Basics

In the Forex market, currency quotes and pips are fundamental concepts that underpin trading and understanding price fluctuations between different currencies. These elements are essential for traders who want to make informed decisions and execute successful trades.

Currency Quotes and Relative Value:

Currency quotes represent the relative value of one currency against another. They are expressed in currency pairs, where the first currency is called the "base currency" and the second is the "quote currency". The exchange rate indicates how many units of the quote currency are needed to buy one unit of the base currency.

For example, if the EUR/USD pair is quoted at 1.2000, it means that 1 euro is worth 1.20 US dollars. Currency quotes reflect the relative strength between two currencies and are influenced by many factors, including economic indicators, monetary policies and global events.

Pips: The Smallest Price Change:

Pips, or "percentage in point", are the smallest possible change in currency prices. They represent the minimum change in the value of a currency pair. On major pairs, most quotes are quoted to four decimal places, with the exception of the Japanese yen, which is quoted to two decimal places.

For example, if the EUR/USD pair rises from 1.2000 to 1.2005, the change is 5 pips. If the USD/JPY pair rises from 110.50 to 110.55, the change is also 5 pips. Understanding pips is crucial for determining position sizes, calculating potential profits and losses, and managing risk effectively.

Importance in Analysis and Execution:

Reading quotes and understanding pips are essential for analyzing and executing trades in the Forex market. Traders use pip movements to identify trends, chart patterns, and entry and exit opportunities. Accuracy in reading quotes is also crucial to avoid errors when executing orders.

Furthermore, knowledge of pips allows traders to calculate the risk-reward ratio, determine stop-loss and take-profit levels, and manage their positions effectively.

Currency quotes and pips are essential fundamentals in the Forex market. Quotes reflect the relative value of currencies in pairs, while pips represent the smallest possible change in prices. Reading quotes and understanding pips are fundamental for technical analysis, risk management and accurate trade execution. Understanding these concepts helps traders make informed and effective decisions in a dynamic, ever-moving market.

3. What is spread and how it affects your trades

Spread in Forex Trading: Understanding the Impact on Business

The spread is a fundamental concept in Forex Trading, as it directly influences the cost of executing operations. It represents the difference between the buy (ask) and sell (bid) prices of a currency pair. The spread is one of the main ways that brokers make money in the Forex market.

Difference between Ask and Bid:

The bid price, also known as the "ask" or "ask price", is the price at which you can buy a currency pair on the market. The ask price, or "bid" or "bid price", is the price at which you can sell the same currency pair. The spread is the difference between these two prices and is usually expressed in pips.

Impact on business:

The spread has a direct impact on trading results. When you enter a position, the price you pay is the ask price. If you want to close the position immediately, you sell at the ask price (bid). So the spread is the initial cost you need to overcome in order for the trade to start making a profit.

Spread Variation:

Spreads may vary depending on market volatility and currency pair liquidity. During times of high volatility, such as major economic announcements, spreads tend to widen, reflecting uncertainty and the greater associated risk. Likewise, less liquid currency pairs may have wider spreads as there are fewer active buyers and sellers.

Choosing a Broker with Competitive Spreads:

Choosing a broker with competitive spreads is crucial for trading results. Tighter spreads reduce the cost of entering and exiting positions, allowing you to reach the profit point faster. However, keep in mind that spreads are not the only consideration when choosing a broker; reliability, regulation, order execution and additional features are also important.

The spread in Forex Trading represents the difference between the buy and sell prices of a currency pair. It directly affects the cost of entering and exiting positions, influencing trading results. Market volatility and currency pair liquidity can cause spreads to vary. Choosing a broker with competitive spreads is a key consideration for optimizing your trading results.

4. Leverage and margin: understanding the risks

Forex Leverage and Margin: Essential Tools and Risks

Leverage and margin are two essential tools in Forex Trading, allowing traders to broaden their exposure to the market and potentially increase their profits. However, it is important to understand that these tools also carry significant risks that require careful management.

Leverage: Expanding Possibilities and Risks

Leverage allows traders to control positions that are larger than their available capital. This is possible because brokers lend an additional amount for every dollar invested by the trader. For example, a leverage of 1:100 means that for every dollar invested, the trader can control a position of 100 dollars. Leverage is a powerful tool for maximizing potential earnings.

Relationship between Leverage and Margin: Amplifying Gains and Losses

Margin, in turn, is the amount of capital that a trader must have available in his account to open a leveraged position. It acts as collateral against potential losses. The higher the leverage, the lower the required margin. While leverage magnifies profit potential, it also magnifies losses as the amount invested is multiplied.

Careful Leverage Management: Protecting Capital

While leverage can be tempting, careful management is crucial to protecting capital. High leverage can expose traders to adverse price movements, leading to rapid and significant losses. A general rule of thumb is never to risk more than you are willing to lose on a single trade.

Importance of Education and Practice:

Before using leverage and margin, traders should invest time in education and practice. Understanding how these tools work, learning how to calculate margins and understanding the associated risks are crucial steps. Practice on demo accounts helps to gain confidence without risking real capital.

Leverage and margin are fundamental tools in Forex Trading, offering the ability to magnify potential gains. However, they also increase the risk of substantial losses. Careful leverage management is essential to protecting capital and maintaining a disciplined approach. Education, practice and a clear understanding of risk are vital components to successfully navigating the Forex market using leverage and margin.

5. Forex market opening hours

Forex Market Hours: A Global Window of Opportunity

Forex market opening hours are a key aspect for traders as it influences the availability of trading opportunities and price volatility. Unlike many other financial markets, Forex operates 24 hours a day, five days a week, due to its global nature and the overlapping time zones of different regions.

Continuous Operation:

The Forex market does not have a centralized physical location. Instead, trading takes place electronically through a global network of banks, financial institutions and individual traders. This allows the market to remain open for most of the week, with the exception of weekends.

Overlapping Trading Sessions:

The overlapping of trading sessions from different regions of the world is a key point to note. When two major sessions overlap, liquidity increases significantly, and this usually happens when the Asian session overlaps with the European session and when the European session overlaps with the North American session. These overlaps can result in increased volatility and trading opportunities.

Main Trading Sessions:

1. Asian Session: Includes Tokyo, Hong Kong and Singapore. While it is the quietest session in terms of volatility, it can often set the tone for the European session.

2. European Session: Centered in London, this is the session with the highest trading volume. Many traders consider this to be the best time to trade due to high liquidity and volatility.

3. North American Session: Includes New York and Toronto. The overlap with the European session creates a period of high activity, further increasing liquidity and volatility.

The Importance of the Overlay Session:

Overlapping trading sessions are an especially important time for traders, as markets in different regions are open simultaneously. This creates a window of time with greater activity and sharper price movements, which can offer profitable opportunities, but also entails additional risks.

Forex market hours are a unique feature that gives traders the flexibility to trade at any time of the day or night, for most of the week. The overlap of trading sessions, with their spikes in liquidity and volatility, is especially important for traders looking for opportunities in different time zones. However, it is critical to understand the risks associated with volatility during these periods and adjust strategies accordingly.

Chapter 3: Fundamental Analysis

1. What is fundamental analysis?

Fundamental Analysis in the Forex Market: Understanding Economic Fundamentals

Fundamental analysis is an essential approach in the Forex market that focuses on evaluating the economic, political and social factors that affect currency exchange rates. In contrast to technical analysis, which relies on chart and historical price patterns, fundamental analysis seeks to understand the underlying fundamentals that drive financial markets.

Evaluation of Economic Factors:

Fundamental analysis examines a range of economic indicators such as interest rates, inflation, economic growth, unemployment and the trade balance. These indicators are used to assess a country's economic health and predict how monetary and fiscal policies may influence exchange rates. For example, a strong economy often attracts foreign investors, increasing demand for the country's currency.

Consideration of Political and Social Factors:

In addition to economic factors, fundamental analysis also considers political and social events that may have an impact on currencies. Political changes, elections, geopolitical crises and other events can create uncertainties that affect exchange rates. For example, an unexpected political event can cause a negative reaction in the markets, leading to a currency devaluation.

Analysis of Interest Rates and Monetary Policies:

Interest rates play a crucial role in fundamental analysis. Changes in interest rates set by central banks can influence capital flows and therefore exchange rates. A higher interest rate in a country can attract investors looking for better returns, increasing demand for the currency.

Importance of Understanding the Fundamentals:

Fundamental analysis is essential for traders who want to make informed decisions in the Forex market. Understanding economic and political fundamentals helps traders anticipate price movements and identify trading opportunities. However, it is important to emphasize that fundamental analysis is not an exact science and requires a careful evaluation of several factors together.

Fundamental analysis is a critical approach to the Forex market, focusing on evaluating the economic, political and social factors that affect currency exchange rates. By considering economic indicators, monetary policies and global events, traders can gain valuable insights into the direction of markets. Understanding the underlying fundamentals is an essential component of making informed and successful Forex trading decisions.

2. Economic indicators that affect the Forex market

Economic Indicators in Forex: Impact on Exchange Rates

Economic indicators play a vital role in the fundamental analysis of the Forex market. They provide insights into a country's economic health and directly influence traders' decisions. Some of the key economic indicators that traders track include Gross Domestic Product (GDP), unemployment rate, inflation and trade balance.

1. Gross Domestic Product (GDP):

GDP is an indicator that measures the total economic output of a country. It reflects the value of all goods and services produced within a nation's borders in a given period. A strong GDP is often associated with a strong currency, as it indicates a robust and growing economy. On the other hand, a weak GDP can lead to currency devaluation.

2. Unemployment Rate:

The unemployment rate indicates the proportion of the labor force that is unemployed and looking for a job. A low unemployment rate is generally positive for the currency, as it suggests a healthy economy and robust demand for goods and services. However, a sudden drop in the unemployment rate can also indicate inflationary pressures, which can affect exchange rates.

3. Inflation:

Inflation measures the general increase in prices of goods and services in an economy. A moderate level of inflation is normal and healthy, but high and uncontrolled inflation can hurt people's purchasing power and negatively affect the currency. Traders look to indicators such as the Consumer Price Index (CPI) to gauge inflationary pressures.

4. Trade Balance:

The trade balance reflects the difference between a country's exports and imports. A positive trade balance, where exports exceed imports, can strengthen the currency, as it indicates a growing demand for the country's products. On the other hand, a deficit in the trade balance can put downward pressure on the currency.

Volatile Impact on Data Release:

The release of these economic indicators often leads to volatile movements in the markets. Traders are keeping an eye on release dates to prepare for potential sudden changes in exchange rates. Markets' reaction may vary depending on how the released data compares to market expectations. If the data beats expectations, the coin could strengthen. If the data falls short of expectations, the currency could weaken.

Economic indicators are key parts of fundamental analysis in the Forex market. GDP, unemployment rate, inflation and trade balance are some of the most influential indicators. They offer insights into a country's economic health and prospects, directly affecting currency exchange rates. The release of this data is often accompanied by volatile movements in the markets, making it essential for traders to understand and monitor these indicators closely.

3. Monetary policy and interest rates

Monetary Policy, Interest Rates, and the Forex Market: A Vital Interconnection

Monetary policy and interest rates play a significant role in the Forex market, as central bank decisions have a direct impact on the value of currencies. The relationship between these factors is complex and crucial for traders to understand.

Central Bank Decisions and Interest Rates:

Central banks are responsible for setting a country's interest rates as part of its monetary policy. Interest rates affect the cost of borrowing and influence the behavior of consumers, businesses and investors. When interest rates are high, the cost of borrowing increases, which can discourage spending and reduce inflation. On the other hand, lower interest rates can stimulate spending and investment.

Impact on the Forex Market:

Central bank decisions regarding interest rates have a direct effect on the Forex market. Increases in a country's interest rates often lead to an appreciation of its currency. This is because higher interest rates attract investors looking for higher yields. These investors can exchange their currency for the one with higher interest rates, increasing the demand for that currency and, consequently, raising its value.

Attracting Investors and Capital Flows:

When a country raises its interest rates, it becomes more attractive to investors looking for more substantial returns on their investments. This capital flow can lead to an appreciation of that country's currency against other currencies. On the other hand, a reduction in interest rates could result in a currency devaluation, as investors may look elsewhere for better opportunities.

Additional Considerations:

It is important to note that the relationship between interest rates and currencies is not always straightforward and can be influenced by many factors such as future expectations, economic stability, geopolitical events and economic indicators. Furthermore, central bank actions can sometimes have a temporary impact before markets adjust to new realities.

Central bank decisions regarding interest rates are a key factor in the Forex market. Increases in interest rates can attract investors looking for higher yields, increasing demand for the currency and, consequently, raising its value. The interconnection between monetary policy, interest rates and currency movements highlights the importance for traders to follow central bank decisions and their repercussions on financial markets.

4. Geopolitical events and their impact on currencies

Geopolitical Events in Fundamental Forex Market Analysis

Geopolitical events play a significant role in the fundamental analysis of the Forex market, as they can cause volatility and abrupt movements in exchange rates. The complex interplay between political, economic and social events in different countries can influence currencies in diverse and unpredictable ways.

Impact of Political Events:

Political events such as elections, government changes and political crises can affect currencies in many ways. Political uncertainty can lead to volatility as investors seek to understand the future implications of political changes. For example, an unexpected election can cause uncertainty about future economic policies, leading to movements in exchange rates.

Influence of Economic Factors:

Economic events such as surprise economic indicators, monetary policy announcements and changes in a country's economic health can also have a profound impact on currencies. Central bank decisions on interest rates and economic stimuli, for example, can generate substantial movements in markets.

International Crisis and Conflict Scenarios:

Economic crises and international conflicts can cause turmoil in financial markets and exchange rates. Investors often seek refuge in currencies considered safe, such as the US dollar and Japanese yen, in times of uncertainty. On the other hand, the currencies of countries involved in conflicts may face pressure due to the associated risk.

Changes in Government Policies:

Changes in government policies, such as regulatory changes, trade policies and enforcement, can directly affect economic prospects and, by extension, currencies. The adoption of more restrictive policies or the imposition of trade tariffs may negatively impact the currencies of the countries involved.

Volatility and Opportunities:

While geopolitical events can generate volatility and risk, they can also create opportunities for experienced traders. Those who are aware of these events can anticipate price movements and adjust their strategies accordingly. However, it is important to remember that geopolitical events are highly unpredictable and can result in rapid and unpredictable movements in markets.

Geopolitical events play a crucial role in the fundamental analysis of the Forex market. The interaction between political, economic and social events in different countries can lead to volatile movements in exchange rates. Traders who understand the influence of these events can capitalize on them, but they must also be prepared to deal with the uncertainty and rapid change they can bring to financial markets.

5. Using fundamental analysis in your trading decisions

Using Fundamental Analysis in Trading Decisions: Practical Guidelines

Using fundamental analysis in trading decisions requires a balanced approach and understanding of the factors that influence currencies. Combining fundamental analysis with other approaches such as technical analysis can provide a more complete and informed view of the Forex market.

1. Understanding of Economic Indicators:

Familiarize yourself with key economic indicators that can affect currencies. This includes GDP, unemployment rate, inflation, trade balance and others. Know which indicators are most relevant for the currency pairs you are trading.

2. Economic Calendar:

Use a reliable economic calendar to track economic data releases and geopolitical events. This will help you prepare for potential volatile movements in the markets and help you make informed decisions.

3. Combining Fundamental and Technical Analysis:

While fundamental analysis is essential, combining it with technical analysis can give you a more complete understanding of the market. Technical analysis involves looking at price patterns, trends and technical indicators. A combined approach can help confirm or refine your decisions.

4. Data Interpretation:

When interpreting economic data, compare it to market expectations. If the data beats expectations, it could lead to a currency appreciation. If the data falls short of expectations, the currency could weaken. Remember that market reaction is not always predictable, so be prepared for different scenarios.

5. Assessment of Geopolitical Events:

When evaluating geopolitical events, consider the potential impact on economic policies and market prospects. Consider how political events, international conflicts or changes in government policies can affect currencies.

6. Risk Management:

Regardless of the approach used, risk management is critical. Set loss limits and position size according to your risk tolerance. Unexpected events can cause sharp movements in the markets, so be prepared to protect your capital.

Example:

Imagine that economic data shows an unexpected increase in a country's GDP. This indicates a strong and healthy economy. Based on fundamental analysis, you can anticipate an appreciation of that country's currency. However, also use technical analysis to confirm the direction of price movement and identify support and resistance levels.

Using fundamental analysis requires an informed approach and understanding of the economic and geopolitical factors that affect currencies. Combining fundamental analysis with technical analysis and proper risk management can help traders make more informed and successful decisions in the Forex market. Always be aware of information and events that can influence exchange rates and adapt your strategies as necessary.

Chapter 4: Basic Technical Analysis

1. Introduction to technical analysis

Introduction to Technical Analysis in the Forex Market: Understanding Patterns and Trends

Technical analysis is a crucial approach in the Forex market, focused on interpreting patterns and trends in price charts to predict future currency movements. While fundamental analysis focuses on economic and geopolitical factors, technical analysis seeks to understand past price behavior as a basis for making informed decisions.

Analyzing Price Charts:

In technical analysis, traders study price charts to identify recurring patterns, trends, and behaviors. Charts show the history of prices over time, and these patterns can provide insight into how prices might behave in the future.

Identification of Patterns and Trends:

Traders use tools like trend lines, moving averages, technical indicators and candlestick formations to identify patterns and trends. Patterns such as heads and shoulders, triangles and flags can indicate reversals or continuation of trends. Trends, in turn, can be upwards (bullish), downwards (downwards) or sideways (consolidation).

Principles of Technical Analysis:

Technical analysis is based on a few fundamental principles:

1. History repeats itself: Technical analysis assumes that patterns and trends that occurred in the past tend to repeat themselves in the future.

2. Prices Reflect Everything: Technical analysis considers that all available information about an asset, including fundamental factors, is already reflected in prices.

3. Mass Behavior: Technical analysis takes into account that price movements are influenced by the collective behavior of traders, creating visible patterns on charts.

Use of Technical Indicators:

Technical indicators are mathematical tools applied to price charts to provide additional information about the trend, strength, momentum and overbought/oversold conditions of an asset. Examples of indicators include RSI (Relative Strength Index), MACD (Moving Average Convergence/Divergence) and Bollinger Bands.

Understanding Price Trends:

Technical analysis helps traders understand whether an asset is in an uptrend, a downtrend, or in a period of consolidation. This understanding is vital for making decisions about opening, closing or managing positions.

Technical analysis is an essential approach in the Forex market, focused on interpreting patterns and trends in price charts. It allows traders to understand past price behavior to predict future currency movements. By combining technical analysis with other approaches such as fundamental analysis, traders can gain a more complete view of the market and make informed decisions about their trades.

2. Candlestick charts: patterns and interpretation

Candlestick Charts in Technical Analysis: Deciphering Price Action

Candlestick charts play a key role in technical analysis, offering a detailed view of price action over time. This visual approach allows traders to identify patterns and trends that can provide valuable insights into future price movements.

Importance of Candlestick Charts:

Candlestick charts are especially important because they not only show the open, close, high and low prices, but also present this information in a visually meaningful way. Each "candle" on the chart represents a specific period of time (for example, an hour, a day) and offers information on how the price behaved during that period.

Interpretation of Candlestick Patterns:

Candlestick patterns are specific configurations formed by the individual candlesticks on a chart. These patterns can indicate possible reversals or continuation of trends. Some common candlestick patterns include:

1. Doji: A doji occurs when the opening price and closing price are nearly identical, resulting in a candlestick with a small body and long tails. It can signal indecision in the market and a possible trend reversal.

2. Hammer: A hammer is a candlestick with a small body and a long lower shadow. It hints at a possible reversal of a downtrend, indicating that buyers are starting to outperform sellers.

3. Shooting Star: A shooting star is the opposite of a hammer, with a small body and a long upper shadow. It could indicate a reversal of an uptrend as sellers are becoming more active.

4. Bullish/Bearish Engulfing: A bullish engulfing pattern occurs when a bullish candle completely "swallows" the previous bearish candle. The reverse is true for a bearish engulfing. It can indicate significant reversals.

5. Head and Shoulders Pattern: This pattern is made up of three peaks, with the center peak (head) being the highest. It can indicate a reversal from an uptrend to a downtrend.

Identifying Patterns and Trends:

Interpreting candlestick patterns is a crucial skill for traders. By identifying patterns like the ones mentioned above, traders can anticipate possible changes in price direction. However, it is important to remember that candlestick patterns are not foolproof and should be considered in conjunction with other information such as technical indicators and longer term trends.

Candlestick charts are an essential tool in technical analysis, allowing traders to decipher price action over time. Interpretation of candlestick patterns such as doji, hammer, shooting star and others helps traders to identify possible reversals or continuation of trends. By using candlestick charts in conjunction with other technical analysis tools, traders can make informed decisions and improve their Forex market trading strategies.

3. Main types of technical indicators

Main Technical Indicators in Technical Analysis

Technical indicators are essential tools in technical analysis, helping traders interpret and make decisions based on historical price data. Here are some of the main types of technical indicators and how they can be applied:

1. Moving Averages:

Moving averages are used to smooth out fluctuations in price data and identify trends. There are two main types of moving averages: simple (SMA) and exponential (EMA). Moving averages can be used to determine trend direction, identify support and resistance, and generate buy or sell signals when they cross other indicators.

2. MACD (Moving Average Convergence/Divergence):

The MACD is an indicator that combines moving averages to identify trend strength and direction. It consists of two lines - the MACD line and the signal line. The interaction between these lines can provide entry and exit signals, as well as indicate divergences between the price and the indicator, which can indicate possible trend reversals.

3. RSI (Relative Strength Index):

The RSI measures the speed and magnitude of price changes, helping to identify overbought and oversold conditions. Ranges from 0 to 100 and values above 70 usually indicate overbought, while values below 30 indicate oversold. The RSI can be used to identify possible trend reversals when divergences between the indicator and prices occur.

4. Stochastic:

The stochastic indicator also helps to identify overbought and oversold conditions, but it compares the current closing price with the price range over a specific period. This creates two lines, %K and %D. Values above 80 usually indicate overbought, while values below 20 indicate oversold. Crossings of the %K and %D lines can provide entry and exit signals.

5. Bollinger Bands:

Bollinger Bands consist of three lines: a simple moving average (usually 20 periods) and two bands that are above and below the moving average, usually one and a half times the standard deviation of prices. The bands expand in periods of high volatility and contract in periods of low volatility. They can be used to identify reversals and entry opportunities when prices touch the bands.

Application and Calculation:

These indicators are calculated based on specific mathematical formulas that take historical prices into account. They can be applied directly to price charts to provide additional information about trends, movement strength and market conditions. Traders can use these indicators in conjunction with other technical analysis tools like candlestick patterns and trendlines to make informed decisions.

Technical indicators play a crucial role in technical analysis, helping traders interpret historical price data and make informed decisions. Moving Averages, MACD, RSI, Stochastic and Bollinger Bands are just a few examples of the available indicators. Applying these indicators can help traders identify trends, strength of movement and overbought or oversold conditions, enhancing their ability to make informed decisions in the Forex market.

4. Support and resistance: identification and use

Support and Resistance in Technical Analysis: Identification and Use

Support and resistance are fundamental concepts in technical analysis that help traders understand the price zones where supply and demand can influence market movements. They are key points on the price chart that play a crucial role in traders' decision making.

Support:

Support is a price level where buying pressure is significant enough to prevent prices from falling further. It acts as a virtual floor at which prices are more likely to stop falling and possibly reverse. Support can be formed based on previous levels where prices found it difficult to fall below.

Resistance:

Resistance, on the other hand, is a level where selling pressure is intense enough to limit price movement upwards. It works as a virtual ceiling at which prices can stop rising or even reverse. Resistance is often formed at points where prices have found it difficult to rise above in the past.

Identification in the Graphics:

To identify support and resistance levels on charts, traders often look for areas where prices stopped rising or falling and made a reversal. This can be done by looking at previous tops and bottoms where prices changed direction. Also, tools like horizontal lines can be used to plot these levels on the chart.

Use in Decision Making:

Support and resistance can be used in several ways when making trading decisions:

- Entry Points: Traders can use support levels as potential entry points for buy positions, as this is where prices are expected to stop falling and could reverse. Likewise, resistance levels can be used as entry points for sell positions.

- Exit Points: Resistance levels can be used as exit points for buy positions, as prices may find it difficult to continue rising. On the other hand, support levels can be used as exit points for sell positions.

- Risk Management: Support and resistance levels can also help traders set stop-loss levels, limiting losses if prices break through these levels.

Support and resistance are fundamental concepts in technical analysis, providing key points on the price chart where buying and selling pressure is significant. Identifying these levels on charts can help traders make informed decisions about entry points, exit points and risk management. Understanding these concepts is crucial to improving Forex trading strategies.

5. Using Trends and Trendlines

Importance of Trends and Use of Trendlines in Technical Analysis

Trends play a key role in technical analysis, providing traders with valuable insights into the general direction of prices and allowing them to identify trading opportunities. Through trend analysis, traders can make informed decisions about when to buy, sell or hold.

Trend Identification:

Trends are patterns of price movement over time. They can be identified by looking at the tops and bottoms on the price chart. Uptrends are characterized by rising tops and bottoms, while downtrends have falling tops and bottoms. Sideways trends occur when prices are moving horizontally with no clear direction.

Influence on Negotiation Decisions:

Different trends have different influences on trading decisions:

- Uptrend: In an uptrend, traders tend to look for buying opportunities, hoping prices will continue to rise. The idea is to buy at pullbacks to take advantage of the uptrend.

- Downtrend: In a downtrend, traders look for selling opportunities, hoping prices will continue to fall. They may look for pullback points to enter short positions.

- Sideways Trend: In a sideways trend, traders can look for short-term moves within the established price range, but they can also choose to wait until a new trend develops.

Using Trend Lines:

Trendlines are tools that help you visualize and confirm the direction of a trend. To identify an uptrend, you can draw a line connecting ascending lows, while for a downtrend, you can connect descending highs. Trendlines can be used to:

- Confirm trend direction.

- Identify possible entry or exit points.

- Predict areas of support and resistance.

Reversals and Breaks of Trend Lines:

A breakout of a trendline can indicate a possible reversal or change in trend direction. However, it is important to confirm these breakouts with other indicators or patterns before making trading decisions.

Trends play a crucial role in technical analysis, guiding traders' buying and selling decisions. Identifying uptrends, downtrends and sideways is essential for an informed approach. Trendlines help visualize and confirm the direction of trends, as well as provide information about potential reversal points and support/resistance areas. By incorporating trend and trendline analysis into their strategy, traders can increase their chances of success in the Forex market.

Chapter 5: Trading Strategies

1. Scalping: short-term strategy

Scalping in the Forex Market: Profiting from Small Price Movements

Scalping is a popular trading strategy in the Forex market that involves performing multiple short-term trades throughout the day with the aim of profiting from small price movements. This approach focuses on capturing small price fluctuations, accumulating gains over time.

Scalping features:

1. Quick Trades: Scalpers open and close positions in a matter of minutes or seconds, taking advantage of intraday price fluctuations.

2. Small Earnings: The strategy seeks to earn small amounts in each operation, relying on the repetition of these operations to increase profits.

3. High Trading Volume: Given the very short-term nature, scalpers can perform dozens or even hundreds of trades in a single day.

4. Focus on Technical Analysis: Scalpers often rely on technical analysis, using indicators and candlestick patterns to identify opportunities.

Advantages of Scalping:

- Less Exposure to Risk: As the operations are short-term, the risk of large price movements against the position is reduced.

- Steady Profits: The strategy aims to accumulate small gains over time, which can be attractive for traders who prefer consistent results.

- Take advantage of Intraday Volatility: Scalping benefits from price fluctuations that occur throughout the day, especially during overlapping trading sessions.

Challenges and Considerations:

- Transaction Costs: Due to the high volume of operations, costs of spreads and commissions can affect profits.

- Technological Requirements: Fast execution of operations requires an efficient trading platform and a reliable internet connection.

- Discipline and Emotions: The frantic nature of scalping requires discipline to follow strict rules and avoid impulsive decisions.

- Risk Control: Rigorous risk management is essential, as a single unfavorable transaction can significantly impact accumulated earnings.

Scalping is a short-term trading strategy that seeks to profit from small price movements in the Forex market. While it can be a profitable approach for experienced traders, it requires fast execution, solid analytical skills and strict discipline to control risk. Those who choose to take up scalping must be prepared to face challenges and adjust their strategies as necessary.

2. Day trading: intraday operations

Day Trading in the Forex Market: Intraday Trades for Quick Profits

Day trading is a popular trading strategy in the Forex market that involves opening and closing positions within the same trading day. Day traders seek to profit from intraday price fluctuations, avoiding holding positions open overnight to avoid possible risks related to events that occur outside of trading hours.

Key Features of Day Trading:

1. Quick Trades: Day traders execute multiple trades in a single day, taking advantage of price movements that occur during trading sessions.

2. Focus on Technical Analysis: Technical analysis is essential to day trading as traders use indicators, candlestick patterns and chart analysis to identify entry and exit opportunities.

3. Constant Monitoring: Day traders need to constantly monitor prices and market conditions to identify potential entry and exit points.

4. Risk Management: Due to the short-term nature of operations, risk management is crucial to protecting capital. Stops and Limits are used to control losses and secure gains.

Importance of Risk Monitoring, Analysis and Management:

- Constant Monitoring: Day trading requires constant attention to market movements. Day traders need to be ready to act quickly when they spot trading opportunities.

- Technical Analysis: Technical analysis helps day traders identify trends, candlestick patterns and entry/exit signals. They rely on charts and indicators to make informed decisions.

- Risk Management: Day trading can be risky due to the volatile and fast paced nature of the trades. Traders need to set suitable stop-loss levels and limits to protect their capital and avoid significant losses.

Advantages of Day Trading:

- Less Exposure to Nighttime Risk: By avoiding holding positions overnight, day traders are less exposed to unforeseen events that may occur outside of trading hours.

- Potential for Quick Profits: Intraday trading allows day traders to seek quick profits based on daily price fluctuations.

- Flexibility: Day trading may be suitable for traders who prefer to keep a close eye on the markets and do not wish to leave positions open overnight.

Challenges and Considerations:

- Stress and Pressure: The fast paced nature of operations can be stressful and require quick decisions.

- Transaction Costs: The number of operations can lead to significant transaction costs in terms of spreads and commissions.

- Experience and Knowledge: Day trading requires a good understanding of the markets, technical analysis and execution skills.

Day trading is a trading strategy involving intraday trading for quick profits. Day traders open and close positions within the same day, avoiding holding positions overnight. Success in this approach depends on constant monitoring of the markets, sound technical analysis and effective risk management. While challenging, day trading can be a viable option for traders who prefer fast action and don't want exposure to overnight risks.

3. Swing trading: taking advantage of short-term trends

Swing Trading: Taking Advantage of Short-Term Trends

Swing trading is a trading strategy that sits between day trading and position trading, seeking to take advantage of short-term trends that can last from a few days to weeks. This approach aims to capture price movements that occur over shorter periods of time than position traders but longer than day traders.

Features of Swing Trading:

1. Intermediate Duration: Swing traders keep their positions open for a period that can range from a few days to a few weeks. This allows them to capture medium-term price movements.

2. Important Technical Analysis: Technical analysis is crucial for swing trading. Traders use indicators, candlestick patterns and chart analysis to identify entry and exit points.

3. Trends and Patterns: Swing traders look for short-term trends and price patterns that may indicate reversals or continuation of movements.

4. Less Stress Compared to Day Trading: Swing trading does not require the same level of constant monitoring as day trading, allowing traders to take a more relaxed approach.

Importance of Identifying Accurate Entry and Exit Points:

- Entry Points: Identifying accurate entry points is critical to swing trading success. Traders look to enter positions when there are indications that a trend is forming or holding.

- Exit Points: Defining exit points is equally important. Swing traders look to exit positions before a trend reversal occurs, protecting their profits.

Risk Management in Swing Trading:

Risk management is essential in swing trading to protect capital and minimize losses:

- Stop-Loss: Swing traders use stop-loss orders to limit losses in case of adverse price movements.

- Appropriately Sized Positions: Determining the proper size of positions based on acceptable risk is crucial to avoid significant losses.

Advantages of Swing Trading:

- Flexible Timing: Swing trading allows traders more flexibility regarding constant monitoring as compared to day trading.

- Take advantage of short-term movements: Swing traders can take advantage of short-term trends without the pressure to act as quickly as day traders.

- Greater Profit Potential: Compared to position trading, swing trading seeks to capture shorter price movements, offering greater profit potential.

Challenges and Considerations:

- Precise Timing: Identifying the right moment to enter and exit positions is crucial to swing trading success.

- Market Fluctuations: Even with an intermediate duration, positions can be affected by unforeseen events.

Swing trading is an intermediate strategy that aims to take advantage of short-term trends in the Forex market. Traders look for price movements that can last anywhere from a few days to weeks, using technical analysis to identify entry and exit points. Risk management is critical to protecting capital while looking to take advantage of medium-term price movements. While it requires less constant monitoring than day trading, swing trading still requires a solid understanding of the market and price trends.

4. Carry trade: Exploring interest rate differences

Carry Trade: Profiting from Interest Rate Differences

The carry trade is a strategy in the Forex market that is based on exploiting the differences in interest rates between different currencies. Traders seek to profit by taking advantage of higher interest rates in one currency and lower interest rates in another. This strategy involves short-term borrowing and investing, allowing traders to capitalize on interest rate discrepancies.

How Carry Trade Works:

1. Choosing Currency Pairs: Traders select currency pairs where the base currency (the one being bought) has a higher interest rate than the quote currency (the one being sold).

2. Borrowing Low Rate Currency: The trader borrows the lowest interest rate currency, usually selling it in the Forex market.

3. Investing in the High Rate Currency: The proceeds from selling the low interest rate currency are then invested in the higher interest rate currency, allowing the trader to earn on the difference in interest rates.

4. Profit from the Rate Difference: As long as the interest rate of the high rate currency remains higher than that of the low rate currency, the trader will gain from the difference, making additional profit.

Associated Risks:

1. Currency Fluctuations: Changes in exchange rates can significantly affect the profits and losses of a carry trade. A devaluation of the high rate currency against the low rate currency could result in losses.

2. Changes in Monetary Policy: Central bank decisions on changes in interest rates can impact the rate differential that initially motivated the carry trade.

3. Liquidity Risk: In times of high volatility, it may be difficult to liquidate positions quickly, leading to unexpected losses.

Advantages of Carry Trade:

- Gain from Interest Rate Differentials: Traders can take advantage of higher interest rates on their positions, earning significant profits.

- Potential for Stable Profits: If conditions remain favorable, the carry trade can result in stable profits over time.

The carry trade is a strategy that exploits differences in interest rates between currencies, seeking to profit from the difference in rates. While this strategy can be profitable, it also carries significant risks such as currency fluctuations and changes in monetary policies. Traders interested in carrying trades should have a solid understanding of economic fundamentals and be prepared to closely monitor changes in financial markets and central bank policies.

5. Breakout and pullback strategies

Breakout and Pullback Strategies in Technical Analysis

Breakout and pullback strategies are popular approaches in technical analysis that traders use to identify entry and exit points in their trades. Both strategies rely on analyzing price patterns and trends to make informed decisions.

Breakout Strategy:

The breakout strategy involves identifying points where prices break through support or resistance levels. These breakout points signal the possibility of a change in trend direction. Traders look to enter positions when a significant breakout occurs, believing that price will continue to move in the direction of the breakout.

Steps for the Breakout Strategy:

1. Identifying Support and Resistance Levels: Traders identify support levels (where prices tend to stop falling) and resistance levels (where prices tend to stop rising).

2. Watching for Breakout Signs: Traders watch for the breakout of these levels. A breakout occurs when the price breaks through a support or resistance level, indicating a possible start of a new trend.

3. Confirmation: It is important to confirm the breakout with other indicators or patterns before entering a position.

Pullback Strategy:

The pullback strategy involves identifying entry opportunities when prices make a temporary comeback after a strong move. In other words, traders take advantage of temporary corrections in a larger trend to enter positions with a better risk-reward ratio.

Steps for the Pullback Strategy:

1. Current Trend Identification: Traders identify the prevailing trend (bull or bear) using technical analysis.

2. Watching for Temporary Returns: After a strong move, traders watch for a temporary correction, or pullback, where price momentarily bounces back against the prevailing trend.

3. Identifying Continuation Signals: Traders look for signs that the prevailing trend will continue after the pullback, such as candlestick patterns or indicators that indicate strength in the trend direction.

Advantages and Considerations:

- Breakout Strategy: Can catch strong moves at the beginning of a new trend. However, false breakouts can occur, resulting in losses.

- Pullback Strategy: Offers opportunities to enter positions with a better risk-reward ratio. However, correctly identifying pullback points requires accurate analysis.

Breakout and pullback strategies are valuable approaches in technical analysis, allowing traders to identify entry and exit opportunities based on price and trend patterns. The breakout strategy focuses on identifying breakouts of support or resistance levels, while the pullback strategy seeks to take advantage of temporary corrections after strong moves. Both strategies require sound technical analysis and proper confirmation to make informed decisions in the Forex market.

Chapter 6: Risk Management and Trader Psychology

1. Importance of risk management

Importance of Risk Management in the Forex Market

Risk management is a fundamental pillar for success in the Forex market. It involves adopting strategies and techniques aimed at protecting the trader's capital and maintaining a sustainable approach to trading. The inherent volatility and unpredictability of the Forex market makes risk management an essential practice to avoid significant losses and maintain active participation in the market.

Reasons for the Importance of Risk Management:

1. Capital Preservation: The main purpose of risk management is to protect the trader's capital. Avoiding excessive losses is crucial for long-term survival in the market.

2. Emotional Control: Risk management helps maintain emotional control. When traders have a solid risk management plan in place, they are less likely to make impulsive decisions based on emotions.

3. Sustainability: Risk management allows traders to maintain a long-term sustainable approach. Even if there are losses, a well-defined risk management plan ensures that operations do not deplete all capital.

4. Flexibility to Adapt: The Forex market is dynamic and can change quickly. A risk management plan allows traders to adapt to changing conditions without compromising their financial position.

Risk Management Techniques:

1. Stop-Loss and Take-Profit: Setting stop-loss (loss limit) and take-profit (profit limit) levels for each operation is essential. This helps limit losses and ensure profits are secured.

2. Appropriate Position Size: Determining position size based on acceptable risk is important to avoid excessive losses on a single trade.

3. Diversification: Do not put all your capital in a single operation. Spreading capital across different currency pairs or assets reduces risk.

4. Leverage Management: Use leverage carefully, avoiding excessive leverage that can amplify both profits and losses.

Risk management is a critical part of any Forex trading strategy. It not only protects the trader's capital, but also promotes a disciplined and sustainable approach to trading the financial markets. Through the use of proper risk management techniques, traders can face market volatility with confidence, minimizing losses and maximizing long-term profit opportunities.

2. How to calculate the proper position size

Calculation of Appropriate Position Size and Risk Management

Calculating the proper position size is a crucial step in risk management as it helps traders control risk and protect invested capital. This practice involves determining the financial amount to be invested in each operation based on the tolerated risk and the risk/reward ratio. Two common approaches to calculating position size are the 1-2% Rule and the risk/reward ratio.

1-2% rule:

The 1-2% Rule suggests that a trader risk no more than 1-2% of his total capital on a single trade. This means that if a trader's total capital is $10,000, he should not risk more than $100 to $200 on a single trade.

Risk/Reward Ratio:

The risk/reward ratio is used to determine whether a trade is potentially viable, considering the possible risk in relation to the expected profit. A trader sets a stop-loss level and a take-profit level before entering a trade. For example, if the stop-loss level is 50 pips away and the take-profit level is 100 pips away, the risk/reward ratio is 1:2. This means that the trader is willing to risk 1 unit of risk to get 2 units of reward.

Importance of the Approach:

1. Capital Protection: Calculating the position size based on tolerated risk helps to protect the trader's capital. Avoiding significant losses on a single trade is critical to long-term survival in the market.

2. Even Risk Distribution: By adhering to the 1-2% Rule or risk/reward ratio, traders spread risk more evenly across trades. This reduces exposure to potential losses.

3. Discipline and Control: Having a disciplined approach to position size helps maintain emotional control. Traders are less likely to take excessive risks or make impulsive decisions.

4. Feasibility Assessment: The risk/reward ratio also helps traders to assess whether a potential trade is viable. If the risk/reward ratio is not favourable, the trade may not be a sensible choice.

Calculating the proper position size is an essential practice in risk management. The 1-2% Rule and risk/reward ratio are valuable tools that allow traders to control risk, protect capital and make informed decisions about the financial amount to invest in each trade. Adopting this approach contributes to an even distribution of risk and to maintaining a disciplined and sustainable trading strategy.

3. Definindo stop-loss e take-profit

Defining Stop-Loss and Take-Profit: Protecting Gains and Limiting Losses

Setting stop-loss and take-profit levels is a fundamental practice in Forex trading operations. These definitions help traders protect their gains, limit losses and maintain a disciplined risk management plan.

Stop-Loss:

Stop-loss is a predetermined level at which a position is automatically closed to limit losses in case of adverse price movements. By setting a stop-loss, traders decide how much they are willing to risk on a trade before exiting it.

Importance of Stop-Loss:

1. Loss Limitation: Stop-loss protects traders against significant losses in case of unforeseen price movements. It prevents a trade from becoming a runaway loss.

2. Emotional Control: Having a predefined stop-loss helps traders maintain emotional control. They don't need to make impulsive decisions in times of volatility.

3. Part of the Strategy: Stop-loss is part of the risk management strategy, helping traders maintain a disciplined and sustainable approach.

Take-Profit:

The take profit is the predetermined level at which a position is closed to secure gains when prices reach a specific target. It is the achievement of profit sought by the trader.

Importance of Take Profit:

1. Ensure Profit: Take Profit helps traders ensure that they exit the trade with a profit when prices reach a target level.

2. Eliminate the Guesswork: Having a preset take-profit avoids the temptation to wait for bigger gains, which can be risky due to market volatility.

3. Keeping Targets: Take profit is an essential part of sticking to a trading plan and achieving planned profit targets.

Definitions Based on Technical Analysis and Objectives:

Setting stop-loss and take-profit levels is influenced by technical analysis such as price patterns, support and resistance levels, and indicators. Traders also consider their trading objectives, risk tolerance and investment profile when setting these levels.

Setting stop-loss and take-profit levels is essential for risk management and successful execution of trading operations. Stop-loss limits losses, protecting capital, while take-profit ensures gains when prices reach defined targets. These definitions are an integral part of a disciplined strategy and are based on technical analysis, trading objectives and risk tolerance.

4. Dealing with Greed and Fear in Trading

Dealing with Greed and Fear in Trading

The trader's psychology plays a crucial role in trading and can influence decisions, strategies and results. Two common emotional issues that traders face are greed and fear, both of which have the potential to negatively affect their trading. However, there are strategies for dealing with these emotions and maintaining a disciplined approach.

Greed:

Greed can drive traders to take excessive risks in pursuit of bigger profits. This can result in impulsive trading and lack of emotional control.

Strategies for Dealing with Greed:

1. Set Realistic Goals: Set realistic profit goals and avoid getting carried away by the temptation of exorbitant earnings.

2. Manage Expectations: Understand that the market is volatile and unpredictable. Accept that not all trades will result in substantial profits.

3. Follow a Plan: Follow a strict trading plan that includes stop-loss and take-profit settings. This helps to avoid impulsive decisions based on greed.

Fear:

Fear can result in hesitation in making decisions or exiting losing positions, leading to greater losses.

Strategies for Dealing with Fear:

1. Education and Preparation: The more a trader understands the markets and strategies, the more confident he will feel in making informed decisions.

2. Loss Limits: Set loss limits (stop-loss) and respect them. This helps to avoid runaway losses and reduces fear of large losses.

3. Rational Analysis: Base your decisions on technical and fundamental analysis rather than emotional reactions. Analysis helps you make more rational decisions.

Keep the Plan:

One of the most effective approaches to dealing with greed and fear is to stick to a disciplined trading plan. The plan should include risk management strategies, stop-loss and take-profit settings, and realistic profit targets. Sticking to the plan reduces the influence of emotions on decisions and helps you stay focused on your trading goals.

Greed and fear are natural emotions that can affect traders, but they can be controlled through conscious and disciplined strategies. Understanding the importance of keeping psychology in check, setting loss limits and following a trading plan helps to reduce the negative effects of these emotions. Keeping a balanced and rational mindset is essential for successful and sustainable trading in the Forex market.

5. Keeping a trading journal

The Importance of the Trading Journal in the Psychology of the Trader

Keeping a trading journal is a valuable practice that plays an essential role in a trader's psychology. This detailed record of trades, decisions and results not only provides a clear view of the trader's performance, but also contributes to the continuous development and improvement of trading skills.

Reasons to Keep a Trading Journal:

1. Performance Evaluation: A trading journal allows traders to objectively evaluate their performance over time. They can analyze successful and unsussuccessful operations, identifying behavioral patterns and areas for improvement.

2. Learning from Experiences: By reviewing the diary, traders can learn from their past experiences. Identifying mistakes made and wrong decisions helps to avoid repetitions in the future.

3. Informed Decision Making: Keeping a record of decisions made during operations provides insight into the reasoning behind them. This helps to improve informed decision-making in the future.

4. Pattern Identification: The trading journal helps to identify recurring behavioral patterns, such as the tendency to act impulsively or ignore warning signs.

5. Continuous Improvement: Based on the analysis of the diary, traders can adjust their trading strategies, approaches and methods, constantly improving their skills.

Contents of the Trading Diary:

An effective trading journal should contain detailed information such as:

- Date and time of the operation.

- Currency pair traded.

- Position size.

- Defined stop-loss and take-profit levels.

- Technical and fundamental analysis that influenced the decision.

- Observations on the market at that time.

- Emotions and thoughts during the operation.

- Results achieved (profit or loss).

Use for Personal Development:

The trading journal is not only a tool for tracking trades, but also a tool for personal development and continuous improvement. By reviewing past entries, traders can learn from their mistakes, identify strengths and weaknesses, and chart a path to becoming more skilled and successful traders.

Keeping a trading journal is a valuable investment in a trader's psychology. It offers deep insights into trader performance, decision making and emotional behavior. By learning from their experiences, traders can evolve and grow, constantly improving their trading skills and achieving sustainable success in the financial markets.

Chapter 7: Trading Platforms and Tools

1. Types of trading platforms

Types of Forex Trading Platforms

In the Forex market, there are different types of trading platforms that offer traders a variety of options to execute their trades efficiently and conveniently. These platforms can be classified into three main categories: web-based, desktop and mobile.

Web Based Platforms:

Web-based platforms are accessed directly through a web browser, with no need to download or install additional software. They offer benefits such as accessibility on any device with an Internet connection and automatic updates.

Functionalities:

- Interactive charts and technical analysis.

- Access to real-time information on prices and quotes.

- Execution of buy and sell orders.

- Risk management tools such as stop-loss and take-profit.

Desktop Platforms:

Desktop platforms are software programs that are installed directly on a computer. They usually offer more advanced features and customization compared to web-based platforms.

Functionalities:

- Detailed and advanced graphics.

- Customizable technical indicators.

- In-depth analytics.

- More stable platform as it does not depend on constant internet connection.

Mobile Platforms:

Mobile platforms are applications that allow traders to trade on mobile devices such as smartphones and tablets. They offer the convenience of trading on the go and instant market access.

Functionalities:

- Intuitive interface optimized for mobile devices.

- Simplified graphics for viewing on smaller screens.

- Real-time notifications on market movements.

- Fast execution of orders with just a few taps.

Choosing the Right Platform:

The choice of trading platform depends on the trader's individual preferences and needs. Some traders prefer the convenience of mobile platforms, while others value the advanced features of desktop platforms. Web-based platforms offer flexibility, allowing traders to access their accounts from anywhere.

The different categories of trading platforms on the Forex market offer a variety of features to suit traders' needs. Whether through web-based, desktop or mobile platforms, traders can leverage detailed charting, technical analysis, order execution and access to market information to make informed decisions and execute their trades efficiently. Choosing the right platform depends on each trader's individual preferences and trading priorities.

2. Use of charts and indicators on platforms

Use of Charts and Indicators on Trading Platforms

Trading platforms offer a variety of features for technical analysis, allowing traders to make informed decisions based on past price patterns and indicators. The use of charts and indicators is an essential part of the trading strategy, offering valuable insights into price direction and market trends.

Graphics Customization:

The platforms allow traders to customize their charts according to their preferences and trading strategies. This includes choosing different time frames such as minutes, hours, days or weeks to view short to long term price movements.

Chart Types:

Traders can choose from several chart types, including line charts, bar charts, and candlestick charts. Candlestick charts are the most popular as they provide detailed information on opening, closing, highs and lows for a single period.

Technical Indicators:

Technical indicators are mathematical tools that traders use to analyze trends, patterns and overbought or oversold conditions in the market. Some common indicators include:

- Moving Averages: Show average prices over a specific time period, smoothing out fluctuations and helping to identify trends.

- RSI (Relative Strength Index): Measures the speed and change of price movements, identifying overbought or oversold conditions.

- MACD (Moving Average Convergence/Divergence): Shows the difference between two moving averages and can signal reversals or continuation of trends.

How Analytics Helps Decisions:

Technical analysis helps traders make informed decisions as it provides information about the direction and strength of trends, entry and exit points, as well as possible reversals. By identifying price patterns, indicator crossovers and support/resistance levels, traders can form a clearer view of the market and take informed action.

The use of charts and indicators on trading platforms is essential for technical analysis, allowing traders to better understand price movements, identify patterns and trends, and make informed decisions. Customizing the charts and choosing suitable indicators are key parts of the trading strategy, contributing to successful and efficient operations in the Forex market.

3. Market orders and pending orders

Market Orders and Pending Orders on Trading Platforms

In the context of trading platforms, market orders and pending orders are fundamental tools for traders to execute their trades effectively and flexibly. Each order type has its own characteristics and purposes, allowing traders to control their positions more precisely.

Market Orders:

Market orders are executed instantly at the current market price. This means that by submitting a market order, the trader is instructing the platform to immediately buy or sell at the best price available in the market at that time.

When to Use Market Orders:

- When the trader wants to enter or exit a position quickly.

- When volatility is high and price is changing rapidly.

Pending Orders:

Pending orders, also known as limit or stop orders, are instructions to buy or sell an asset at a specific price in the future. Such orders are executed only when the price reaches the level specified by the trader.

Types of Pending Orders:
- Buy Limit Order: Set below the current price, waiting for a drop in price to enter.
- Sell Limit Order: Set above the current price, waiting for the price to rise to enter.
- Buy Stop Order: Set above the current price, activated when the price rises and reaches the specified level.
- Sell Stop Order: Set below the current price, activated when the price drops and reaches the specified level.
When to Use Pending Orders:
- When the trader wants to enter or exit a position at a specific price.
- When there is an expectation of a price change, but the trader is not available to monitor the market.
Importance of Understanding Orders:

Understanding the available order types is crucial to managing positions effectively. Using market orders or pending orders at the right time can help ensure that trades are executed as per the trader's strategy. The choice of order type depends on market conditions, trader preferences and trading objectives.

Market orders and pending orders are essential tools on trading platforms, allowing traders to execute trades flexibly and accurately. Understanding the difference between these types of orders and knowing when to use them is critical to successful trading, ensuring that positions are executed as per the trader's strategy and market conditions.

4. Automation of trading with robots (EAs)

Automated Trading with Robots (EAs) - Expert Advisors

Trading robots, also known as Expert Advisors (EAs), are software programs designed to automate the execution of trades in the Forex market.

They operate based on predefined rules and algorithms, allowing traders to implement trading strategies automatically and continuously.

How EAs work:

EAs analyze market data such as prices, volumes and technical indicators and make buy or sell decisions based on programmed rules. They can execute orders instantly without human intervention, which is especially useful for operations that require speed and precision.

Benefits of Trading Automation:

1. Precise Execution: EAs execute trades according to predefined rules, eliminating human errors and emotions in trading.

2. 24/5 Activity: EAs can operate 24 hours a day, all week, taking advantage of opportunities in different time zones.

3. Quick Analysis: Robots can analyze large volumes of data in a short amount of time, identifying patterns and opportunities that would be difficult for a human trader to follow.

4. Discipline: EAs strictly follow the defined rules, avoiding impulsive or emotional decisions.

Trading Automation Challenges:

1. Complex Development: Creating an EA requires programming skills and a deep understanding of trading strategies.

2. Need for Adjustments: Trading strategies may need constant adjustment as market conditions change.

3. Technological Risks: Technical problems such as Internet connection failures or software errors can lead to losses.

Importance of Testing and Tuning EAs:

Before deploying an EA on a live trading account, it is crucial to test it on a demo account to evaluate its performance. Traders should consider different market scenarios, make adjustments to the settings and optimize the rules to improve the robot's effectiveness. Furthermore, monitoring the EA's performance over time and adjusting as needed is critical to ensuring consistent results.

Trading robots, or Expert Advisors, offer an automated way to implement trading strategies in the Forex market. While they offer benefits such as accurate execution and continuous uptime, they also present challenges in terms of development, tuning and monitoring. Testing and tuning EAs is critical to ensure they meet expectations and deliver consistent results over time.

5. The importance of continuing education about platforms

The Importance of Ongoing Education on Trading Platforms

Ongoing education on trading platforms is essential for traders who want to stay current and get the most out of the tools and resources on offer. Trading platforms not only provide access to the market, but also constantly evolve to meet the ever-changing needs of traders. Here's the importance of staying educated on these platforms:

Platform Evolution:

Trading platforms are constantly evolving to adapt to market demands and technological changes. New functionalities, tools and resources are frequently added to improve the user experience and offer greater efficiency in the execution of operations.

Make the Most of the Tools:

Understanding and making the most of the tools and features offered by the trading platform can result in more informed and successful trades. Features such as advanced charts, technical indicators, price alerts and detailed analysis can help traders make more informed decisions.

Adaptation to Market Changes:

Financial markets are dynamic and subject to rapid change. A well-educated trading platform allows traders to adjust to new trends, economic events and changing market conditions effectively.

Prevention of Errors and Losses:

Continuous education helps prevent mistakes made due to lack of knowledge about the platform. Avoiding execution errors, incorrect order setup and improper use of resources can help to avoid unnecessary losses.
Update on New Features:

As new functionality is added to the platform, educated traders can explore these tools to improve their trading strategy. This may include technical analysis improvements, integration of additional indicators and chart customization.

Ongoing education on trading platforms is critical to keeping pace with technological changes and market developments. Traders who stay informed and up-to-date on available tools and resources can make more informed decisions, avoid mistakes, and make the most of trading opportunities. Constant learning allows traders to be in an advantageous position to navigate the challenges and opportunities of the Forex market.

Chapter 8: Developing a Trading Plan

1. Why a trading plan is essential

Importance of a Forex Trading Plan

Having a trading plan is one of the fundamental pillars for a successful trader in the Forex market. It is a detailed framework that guides a trader's actions and decisions, providing a systematic and disciplined approach to meeting market challenges. Here is the importance of having a trading plan:
Structure for Decisions:

A trading plan sets out clear rules on how to enter and exit positions, how much to risk on each trade, and how to manage capital. This creates a logical framework that guides trading decisions and minimizes the influence of impulsive or emotional decisions.

Discipline and Focus:

A trading plan helps traders stay disciplined and focused on their strategies. It acts as a guide that prevents traders from deviating from their strategies due to emotional fluctuations or market movements. This is key to maintaining a consistent approach and avoiding mistakes caused by impulsiveness.

Reduction of Emotional Impact:

The Forex market is volatile and can often be emotionally challenging. A trading plan helps to reduce the impact of emotions as decisions are based on predetermined rules and objective analysis. This helps to avoid hasty decisions or decisions that are overly influenced by fear or greed.

Adequate Risk Management:

A trading plan includes clear guidelines on risk management, such as position size, stop-loss and take-profit levels. This helps to protect the trader's capital and ensure that significant losses are controlled.

Learning and Improvement:

A trading plan also allows traders to track and evaluate their performance over time. This provides an opportunity to learn from mistakes, adjust strategies as needed, and continually improve.

A trading plan is an essential tool for any trader looking for success and consistency in the Forex market. It provides a solid framework for decision making, maintains discipline and focus, reduces the impact of emotions and helps with risk management. Having a trading plan not only increases the chances of success, but also provides a systematic and strategic approach to meeting market challenges.

2. Key Elements of a Trading Plan

Key Elements of an Effective Trading Plan

An effective trading plan is a detailed guide that guides the trader through every step of the trading process. It contains essential elements that provide clear guidelines for making informed and consistent decisions. Here are the main elements that make up a well-structured trading plan:

1. Trading Strategies:

Define the strategies you will use to enter and exit positions. This includes methods of technical analysis, fundamental analysis or a combination of both. Describe how you will identify trading opportunities and what indicators or patterns you will use to make decisions.

2. Risk Management Rules:

Define clear rules to manage the risk of your operations. This involves determining your position size based on your equity, setting stop-loss and take-profit levels, and setting limits on how much you are willing to risk on a single trade.

3. Entry and Exit Criteria:

Specify the specific criteria that will determine when to enter a position (entry points) and when to exit it (exit points). This may involve price levels, technical indicators, candlestick patterns or other factors relevant to your strategy.

4. Monitoring and Evaluation Plan:

Develop a plan to track and evaluate the performance of your operations. This includes keeping a detailed trading diary, recording the reasons behind each decision, and analyzing the results to identify areas for improvement.

5. Psychology of the Trader:

Include considerations for how you will deal with emotions during the negotiation. Developing a disciplined and controlled mindset is key to avoiding impulsive or overly emotional decisions.

6. Adaptation Plan:

Recognize that the market is constantly changing and that your strategy may need to adjust over time. Develop a plan to regularly evaluate your strategy and make adjustments as needed.

7. Backtesting and Simulation:

Before applying your plan to a live account, test it using historical data to see how it would have performed in the past. This helps to identify potential failures and improve your strategy.

Clarity and Consistency:

Clarity is key in all elements of the trading plan. The clearer and more detailed the plan, the easier it will be to follow the rules and maintain consistency. This helps to avoid mistakes caused by misinterpretations or impulsive decisions.

An effective trading plan is an essential tool to guide the trader through all stages of trading. It provides a clear set of rules for making informed and controlled decisions, managing risk, setting entry and exit criteria, tracking performance and maintaining a disciplined mindset. Clarity and understanding of each element of the plan is vital to success in the Forex market.

3. Setting realistic and achievable goals

The Importance of Setting Realistic and Achievable Goals in the Trading Plan

Setting realistic and achievable goals is a crucial component of a successful trading plan. Goals provide a sense of direction, motivation and a clear framework to guide the trader's actions. Here is the importance of having defined goals in the trading plan:

1. Focus and Direction:

Clear goals help traders to focus on specific goals. They provide a clear purpose for each operation and help to avoid impulsive actions that could compromise the strategy.

2. Measurement of Progress:

Established goals allow traders to measure their progress over time. This allows them to assess whether they are achieving their desired goals and identify areas that need adjustment.

3. Risk Management:

Setting risk targets helps to avoid excessive losses and maintain discipline in risk management. Establishing a maximum loss limit in relation to the total capital can prevent catastrophic results in case of a sequence of unfavorable operations.

4. Profit Goals:

Realistic and achievable profit targets provide a sense of accomplishment and satisfaction when achieved. They also help to avoid greed by allowing traders to exit positions when they reach defined targets.

5. Continuous Learning:

In addition to financial goals, learning goals are also important. This includes goals to improve analytical skills, better understand markets or explore new strategies. Learning goals encourage constant growth and pursuit of knowledge.

6. Reduction of Impulsivity:

Having predefined goals reduces the likelihood of making impulsive decisions. Traders are more likely to stick with their strategy when they have specific goals in mind.

7. Adaptation and Evaluation:

Targets can also be used to assess performance and adapt strategy. If a goal is not being met, it may indicate a need to adjust the approach or strategy.

Setting realistic and achievable goals in the trading plan is essential for success in the Forex market. Goals provide a clear guide to guide the trader's decisions and actions, measure progress over time, and maintain discipline in pursuit of goals. By incorporating financial and learning goals, traders can build a strategic and sustainable approach to their trading activities.

4. Adjusting the trading plan as needed

Adjusting the Trading Plan as Needed

A trading plan is a valuable tool, but it is not a hard and fast rule that must be blindly followed. It must be flexible and adaptable to keep up with changes in the market and the trader's strategies. Here is the importance of adjusting the trading plan as needed:

1. Market Changes:

Financial markets are constantly evolving. Economic conditions, geopolitical events and other variables can influence market dynamics. A trading plan must be adjusted to suit these changes and take advantage of the opportunities that arise.

2. Strategies Evaluation:

It is important to regularly review the strategies included in the trading plan. If a strategy isn't working as expected or isn't generating the desired results, it may need to be adjusted or replaced with another approach.

3. Lessons Learned:

The trading journal is a valuable tool for evaluating performance and learning from past trades. If a decision has not produced the expected results, it is an opportunity to identify mistakes and lessons learned to avoid repetitions in the future.

4. Changing Personal Circumstances:

Changes in financial situation, time availability or personal goals may require adjustments to the trading plan. It is important that the plan remains realistic and achievable given the trader's circumstances.

5. Constant Learning:

As traders gain more knowledge and experience, they can develop new perspectives and approaches. A trading plan should evolve with learning and incorporate new, more effective strategies or tactics.

6. Adaptation to Different Market Conditions:

An effective trading plan must be able to handle different market conditions such as trending markets, volatile markets or sideways markets. Adjustments allow the plan to adapt to current conditions to maximize opportunities.

7. Flexibility Without Losing Focus:

Flexibility is important, but it must be balanced with maintaining focus on the core strategy. Adjustments should be made deliberately and informedly, avoiding frequent changes that could undermine consistency.

A flexible and adaptable trading plan is essential for success in the Forex market. Adjusting the plan as needed allows traders to adapt to market changes, improve their strategies and incorporate lessons learned. The ability to keep a plan up to date and relevant is critical to an effective and sustainable approach to negotiation.

5. Continuous evaluation and improvement of the plan

Continuous Assessment and Improvement of the Trading Plan

Continuous evaluation and improvement of the trading plan are critical elements for long-term success in the Forex market. The dynamic nature of financial markets requires traders to always be willing to learn, adapt and improve their strategies. Here is the importance of this process:

1. Analysis of Results:

The evaluation of the results of operations is fundamental to understand the performance of the trading plan. Identifying which strategies are working well and which ones need tweaking helps guide future actions.

2. Record of Errors and Successes:

Keeping a detailed record of trades, including the reasons behind decisions, helps traders learn from mistakes and successes. This allows them to identify behavioral patterns, recurring mistakes and missed opportunities.

3. Constant Learning:

The Forex market is always evolving. New strategies, indicators and approaches emerge regularly. The pursuit of constant learning allows traders to explore and incorporate innovative ideas into their strategy.

4. Adaptation to Changes:

Markets are subject to economic, political and social changes. A trading plan must be flexible enough to adapt to these changes and take advantage of emerging opportunities.

5. Improvement of Weaknesses:

Continuous assessment helps to identify weaknesses in the trading plan, whether related to strategies, risk management or decision making. Improving these areas contributes to a more solid and effective approach.

6. Focus on Long-Term Goals:

Through continuous evaluation and improvement, traders can focus on long-term goals rather than chasing immediate profits. Sustainable success requires a disciplined and evolutionary approach.

7. Adaptation to Different Market Conditions:

Continuous evaluation allows traders to adjust their plan to suit different market conditions such as volatile, trending or sideways markets. This helps optimize performance in varying scenarios.

Ongoing evaluation and improvement of the trading plan is essential to staying relevant and effective in the Forex market. The ability to analyze results, learn from mistakes and successes, and adapt to market changes is critical to long-term success. Constant strategy evolution is the key to becoming a more skilled and successful trader.